THE MUSUBI BOOK

THE MUSUBI BOOK

Manabu Asaoka
ILLUSTRATIONS BY MARIA ASAOKA

© 2018 Manabu Asaoka

Copyrights on artwork are retained by contributors

All rights reserved. No part of this book may be reproduced in any form or by any electronic or mechanical means, including information retrieval systems, without prior written permission from the publisher, except for brief passages quoted in reviews.

ISBN 978-1-948011-03-7

Library of Congress Control Number: 2018935535

Design and production by Mae Ariola

Photography by Manabu Asaoka except where otherwise noted

Illustrations by Maria Asaoka except where otherwise noted

Legacy Isle Publishing
1000 Bishop St., Suite 806
Honolulu, HI 96813
www.legacyislepublishing.net
info@legacyislepublishing.net

Printed in Korea

This book is dedicated to:

FUMIYO ASAOKA, my wife, whose skills as a licensed nutritionist, co-manager and technical supervisor have been invaluable in creating our business and this book.

MARIA ASAOKA, my niece, a talented illustrator.

MACO ASAOKA, my niece, who served as the hand model for this book.

MARC INOUYE, my close friend, a former Hawaii Pacific University classmate and marketing specialist who suggested that I should publish a musubi book and introduced me to my publisher.

MY FORMER & CURRENT STAFF — Thank you for working hard together to achieve our goal of expanding musubi culture.

OUR CUSTOMERS — Thank you for loving our handmade musubi and supporting our musubi deli business for a decade.

ALL MUSUBI LOVERS — Thank you for helping grow appreciation for musubi worldwide!

TABLE OF CONTENTS

INTRODUCTION	8
CHAPTER ONE: What are Musubi?	10
Musubi History	13
Main Ingredients for Musubi	17
CHAPTER TWO: About Rice	20
Two Categories of Rice	22
Japan: The Land of Japonica	24
Japonica in the U.S.	26
What Makes Tasty Rice?	28

CHAPTER THREE: Things to Know Before Cooking Rice	30
Types of Rice Cookers	32
Water is Important!	34
Measuring Cups	35
Rice Paddles	36
CHAPTER FOUR: How to Make the Best Rice for Musubi	38
Always Use Freshly Cooked Rice!	39
CHAPTER FIVE: Let's Make Fillings!	44
Traditional Japanese Musubi Fillings	48
Contemporary Japanese Musubi	51
American Favorites for Musubi	56
Global Cuisine Musubi	59
CHAPTER SIX: Let's Make Musubi!	68
Equipment	69
Ingredients	70
The Procedure	72
CHAPTER SEVEN: Beyond Basic Musubi (Mixed Rice and Pilaf)	80
Mixed Rice Musubi	80
Pilaf Musubi	86
CHAPTER EIGHT: Musubi on the Go!	92
GLOSSARY	96
ABOUT THE AUTHOR & ILLUSTRATOR	106

INTRODUCTION

"Do you have chopsticks?"
"Is this salmon cooked?"
"Don't you have *wasabi* packets?"

When my wife, Fumiyo, and I opened Mana-Bu's, a small *musubi* boutique on busy South King Street in Honolulu, Hawaii, many first-time customers asked us those questions. Although it was something we hadn't anticipated when we started our business, we gradually learned that some customers confused musubi with *sushi*.

Sushi is the most famous Japanese rice dish in the world, known for its sophisticated preparation and reputation for freshness and healthiness. There are numerous sushi places in America, from upscale sushi bars in big cities to tiny sushi to-go shops in small neighborhoods, and this phenomenon can also be seen in Latin America, Europe, all around Asia, Oceania, and even Africa. We should rejoice that today, sushi restaurants are not exclusively managed by Japanese, but owned and operated by sushi chefs from all backgrounds.

Meanwhile, apart from the Aloha State where it is a local staple, musubi largely remain an unfamiliar food outside of Japan. But musubi have a much longer history than sushi, and they are commonly and frequently eaten throughout Japan by everyone, from kindergarten children to senior citizens. Because of their simple preparation and ability to hold up to a day of being carried in a lunch box, musubi are essential to the home cook's repertoire. Mothers often make musubi in the early morning for their families' lunches, and musubi have become iconic as a food that recalls the "taste of Mom's cooking." At the same time, an enormous number of food vendors also sell musubi commercially, so this "home food" has crossed over into the retail market.

As a result of the happy business experience at our musubi boutique in Hawaii, a melting pot of different races and cultures, Fumiyo and I strongly believe that musubi have the potential to go global in a big way. Musubi easily adapt to a region's own ingredients and tastes. You can see this in the way that Hawaii's famous and iconic SPAM® musubi developed from the Islands' unique food culture.

In this book, I will introduce you to musubi history, culture, statistics and, of course, the essentials of musubi-making—from choosing a rice cooker to recommended wrapping materials—and musubi recipes. I hope all my readers, their families and friends try musubi making and enjoy it as much as I do!

Aloha,
Manabu Asaoka

CHAPTER ONE

WHAT ARE MUSUBI?

Musubi are a type of rice dish, brought to the United States in the late nineteenth century by Japanese immigrants. They are especially popular in Hawaii, but have spread throughout America. A musubi consists of a handful of cooked rice shaped into a triangle or rectangle, with some seasonings, fillings and/or toppings. Like sandwiches, musubi were originally a homemade dish, not something you bought. Musubi have always been loved because they are so convenient for lunch at work or school, picnics, sporting events or field trips. Musubi are usually four to six ounces (one-quarter to three-eighths of a pound), easily held in one hand—even by kids! An average serving would be two to four musubi for children, while adults would be satisfied with three to six.

In Japan, musubi (more commonly called "*o-musubi*" or "*o-nigiri*" in that country, see sidebar) are found everywhere. They are in convenience stores, supermarkets, small grocery stores and even in department stores, where the entire basement floor is devoted to a food market called *depachika*. There are even specialty musubi delicatessens!

MUSUBI, O-MUSUBI OR O-NIGIRI?

You may have heard someone say "o-musubi" instead of "musubi." Or, if you have been to Japan, you may have seen signs that say "o-nigiri" instead of "o-musubi" or "musubi." What's the difference? Well, they are all the same!

In Japan, people don't use the word "musubi." In fact, many people would not understand what the word refers to. When Japanese immigrants brought the o-musubi to America, as they adapted from Japanese to English language, they dropped the "o" from the beginning of the word. Interestingly, the very first use of the word, in the Muromachi era (mid-fourteenth to mid-sixteenth centuries), was "musubi"—the "o" was added in the Edo era to make the word sound more polite. It is a little funny that modern Japanese do not recognize this original form of the word.

"O-nigiri" is even more common in Japan than use of "o-musubi." A survey reported in 2013 that 89% of Japanese speakers say "o-nigiri." "O-musubi" was found to be used more by older residents and people in Yamaguchi and Hiroshima prefectures. This makes sense because these areas are where most of Hawaii's Japanese immigrants came from, and they would have likely brought the word—"o-musubi"—that they were more familiar with.

MUSUBI HISTORY

Musubi are believed to have originated more than two millennia ago. In 1987, an approximately 2,000-year-old fossilized rice ball was discovered at the Chanobatake ruins on the Noto Peninsula, a piece of land that projects from Honshu Island into the Sea of Japan. This is the oldest evidence of people making and eating rice balls. Following this discovery, similar fossilized rice balls were discovered in other regions of Japan, leading historians to conclude that musubi originated in the Iron Age (300 BC–300 AD). Researchers determined that these ancient musubi were made from sticky *mochi* rice and were made by steaming, not boiling, the rice. They also concluded that the musubi were most likely used as offerings for religious purposes.

Rice was a valuable ingredient, and has been consumed as a porridge for a very long time. In the late Heian era (around the twelfth century), rice was widely cultivated throughout Japan, and people started to eat rice in its more intact form, as we see today, instead of as porridge. People began making rice balls, early musubi, as a portable food to carry to the battlefield. They ate their musubi with some salt or *miso* paste for seasoning. From the Kamakura era to the Sengoku era (late twelfth to seventeenth centuries), a period of continued domestic wars, musubi grew in popularity as a battlefield food.

As the production of Japonica rice increased (more on this in the next chapter), musubi shifted from being made with mochi rice to Japonica. People also began to add *umeboshi* (pickled plum) or other salted vegetables to the rice to help preserve it, and to make the musubi more flavorful. The rice was mostly brown rice, but some records show that soldiers were provided with white rice musubi on battle days so they would quickly absorb carbohydrates.

In the Edo era (seventeenth through nineteenth centuries), the Tokugawa shogunate maintained domestic peace. People enjoyed traveling around the country to visit shrines, Buddhist temples and hot springs. Musubi became popular as a portable food for those travelers. Farmers also packed musubi for their lunches in the fields.

In the Meiji era, the beginning of modern Japan, railroads were rapidly built all over the country. With the increase in domestic travel, musubi became more common as a travel-ready food, and local manufacturers started offering unique musubi using regional ingredients. At the same time, the government started compulsory education, requiring children to bring lunches—musubi were perfect to meet this need. During the modern war era, in the nineteenth and twentieth centuries, musubi were widely consumed by soldiers, travelers, students and workers because of their convenience as a portable food.

Today, although there are a lot of other options, such as bread and many varieties of noodles, musubi are still one of the most common and popular staple dishes in Japan, not only as an on-the-go meal, but also as an easy-to-eat snack. Musubi are a top choice for picnics, school or work trips, and lunches for adults and children. Like sandwiches, musubi are widely available in stores everywhere, making it an accessible, popular item. Workers usually buy musubi for lunch or snacks on their way to work, on their lunch break or even late at night. At any casual gathering, musubi will be found since they are so easy to make or buy, and very affordable. From children to senior citizens, everyone loves musubi!

WHAT ARE MUSUBI?

SO, WHAT ABOUT SUSHI?

Sushi is another Japanese rice-based dish, more familiar in America than musubi. The form of sushi we know today is called *nigiri sushi*, with some seafood on top of a tiny rice ball. It originated more than 1,000 years ago in the form of fermented seafood prepared with salt and rice. This original form was called *narae sushi*, and it was made as a means of preserving food.

    During the peaceful Edo era, as Japanese cuisine advanced, people began combining brewed vinegar with fresh seafood instead of waiting for the natural fermentation process. In Tokyo (called Edo at that time) in the early nineteenth century, a chef developed a new style of sushi with cooked seafood on top of a vinegar-seasoned rice ball. This is considered the very first nigiri sushi, the ancestor of today's style. It quickly became very popular, and immediately spread all over Edo. It was served mostly at mobile stands, and the size of each piece of sushi was much larger than the current style—reportedly, it was musubi-sized!

    In the twentieth century, with the development of refrigeration, cooks began putting raw seafood on the vinegar-seasoned rice. Sushi making evolved to a profession, the size of the pieces became smaller, and sushi chefs invented a wider variety of toppings. After WWII, the sophisticated new sushi style spread all over Japan, and it is now considered the definition of "sushi." As Japan's global economic presence expanded, sushi has gone international and is eaten by people all over the world.

MAIN INGREDIENTS FOR MUSUBI

Most musubi are made of white rice because of the medium-level stickiness of the rice grains. Brown rice grains are too dry to hold the musubi shape, while sweet rice (also known as mochi rice) is very difficult to handle because it is so very sticky.

There are three ways to season plain white rice to make it more tasty and enjoyable:

1

Add flavorful fillings in the center of the musubi, and wrap the whole musubi with a sheet of *nori*.

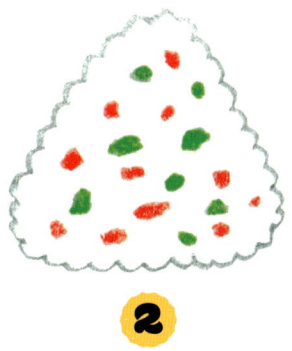

2

Mix the rice with strongly flavored seasonings such as *furikake*; do not wrap with nori.

3

Instead of plain white rice, use a pilaf-style rice; do not wrap with nori.

WHAT ARE MUSUBI?

The first method is the most common way to prepare musubi. The second and third techniques are very good for creating new styles and flavors of musubi, as well as interesting visual presentations. These two methods are also easy for people who aren't as skilled at wrapping musubi with nori!

Unless you are making a musubi with pilaf-style rice, the ingredients are simple:

- White rice
- Water
- Sea salt
- Your favorite fillings or rice seasonings
- Nori (not necessary for the seasoned-rice style)

See how simple musubi are?!

MUSUBI VS. SUSHI

The histories of musubi and sushi are very different. However, outside Japan, the two are frequently mixed up. Sushi is more widely known, so people who encounter musubi are occasionally confused whether their musubi has wasabi or *shoyu*, which would be unthinkable in Japan. To avoid such misunderstandings, here are the basic differences between musubi and sushi:

	 **Musubi**	 **Nigiri Sushi**
Appearance:	Fully or partly wrapped with nori (sometimes served without nori)	Some protein topping on a small rice ball (sometimes nori is used to bind topping and rice)
Shape:	Usually triangular	Rounded rectangle
Amount of Rice:	A handful	Two tablespoons
Seasoning:	Lightly salted rice	Lightly vinegar-seasoned rice or non-seasoned topping
Filling/Topping:	Strongly flavored fillings that are cooked	Raw seafood is commonly used
How to eat:	Hold it in your hand(s), take as many bites as you need	Pinch it in three fingers or use chopsticks, eat in a single bite
Extra spices:	Not used	Wasabi is commonly added
Extra seasoning:	Not used	Shoyu is usually added before eating
Where is it sold in America?	Musubi specialty shops, Japanese delicatessens (*okazuya*), Asian grocery stores	Sushi bars/restaurants, take-out sushi stores & okazuya, Asian grocery stores
Requires refrigeration?	No	Yes
How long does it last?	Half day at room temperature	Should be eaten right away
One adult serving:	3 to 5 pieces	8 to 15 pieces
Average cost per serving:	$5 to $10	$10 to $40

CHAPTER TWO

ABOUT RICE

Rice is one of the three major staple foods in the world.

While European, North American and West Asian people have wheat, and Middle American, South American, South African and some Eastern European people have corn as their principal carbohydrates, East Asian, Southeast Asian and South Asian people historically have eaten rice as their primary food.

WHEAT
European, North American and West Asian staple

CORN
Middle American, South American, South African and some Eastern European staple

RICE
East Asian, Southeast Asian and South Asian staple

Wheat and corn are usually first processed into flour and then that flour is mixed with liquid (water or milk), fat (butter or oil) and seasonings (salt), and then it is baked or boiled. Rice can also be made into flour and then turned into noodles, such as rice vermicelli (in China) and pho (in Vietnam). However, keeping the grains whole and simply boiling or steaming them is the more common method of preparation in East Asian countries such as China, Korea and Japan.

TWO CATEGORIES OF RICE

Scholars say that there are tens of thousands of different kinds of rice in the world. However, recent studies show that rice can be largely divided into just two categories, Japonica and Indica.

Japonica rice first emerged about 8,000 to 9,000 years ago, along the Yangtze Valley in ancient China and was cultivated as a food crop. As rice farming gradually spread to the neighboring regions, such as India and Southeast Asia, the Japonica rice gene was also changed by mixing with other plants. Thus, about 3,900 years ago, a new rice category, Indica, was born in India.

Japonica | | Indica

Japonica		Indica
Short grain. Shorter and rounder than Indica.	**Grain Shape**	Long grain
Temperate Zone (farther from the equator)	**Growing Region**	Subtropical Zone and the Tropical Zone (around the equator)
Tender and sticky	**Texture**	Dry and crunchy
Sweeter	**Flavor and Taste**	Stronger, aromatic flavors (such as jasmine rice)
Less protein and amylose	**Protein and Amylose** (fluffiness & stickiness)	More protein and amylose
Served plain, simply boiled or steamed with water	**How It's Eaten**	Boiled or baked with other ingredients and seasonings, or made into rice flour and used for noodles or wrappers
Preferred in Northern China, Japan and Korea	**Consumption**	Consumed in other rice regions

Market Volume

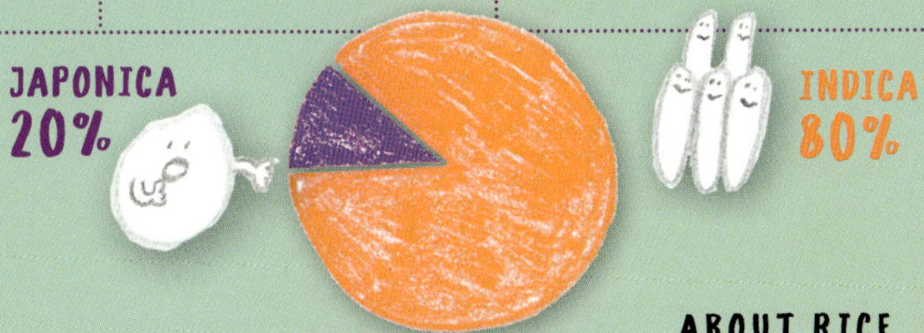

JAPONICA 20%

INDICA 80%

ABOUT RICE 23

JAPAN: THE LAND OF JAPONICA

In 1903, the Japanese government launched a national project at their agricultural experimental station aimed at improving and increasing rice production. The goal was to find rice species that produced many grains, could be easily harvested and were hardy against cold temperature, plant diseases and insect pests. Soon after the project began, instead of growing new plants by taking cuttings of the parent plant, the researchers started growing new plants through pollination. The first new rice species created this way was developed in 1921, and the new method accelerated the speed of developing new rice species. After World War II, the study also included taste as a high priority. Many new tasty species continue to emerge and gain popularity among consumers. The Japanese Ministry of Agriculture, Forestry and Fisheries (MAFF) states that more than 700 rice species have been developed since the program began.

According to MAFF, about 300 species of rice are currently harvested in Japan. Although each rice species has a preferred region and climate, the Koshihikari variety is the most widely harvested and consumed in Japan, with a 36% market share in 2015. Here is more information on the most popular types of rice grown in Japan:

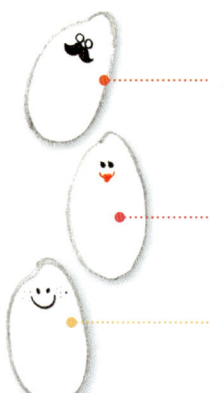

KOSHIHIKARI: Originally developed in 1956, it has 11 improved versions designed to strengthen the plant's tolerance against rice blight. **(36.1% market share)**

HITOMEBORE: A Koshihikari crossbreed developed in 1991 to be more cold-climate tolerant. **(9.7% market share)**

HINOHIKARI: A Koshihikari crossbreed developed in 1989 to be more tolerant of warm climates. **(9.0% market share)**

THE MUSUBI BOOK

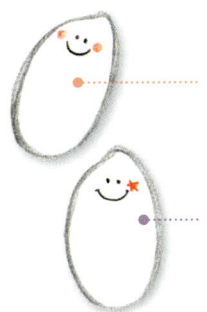

AKITAKOMACHI: This Koshihikari crossbreed was created in 1984 to develop a species that could be harvested earlier in Northern Japan. **(7.2% market share)**

NANATSUBOSHI: This seventh generation of Koshihikari was created in 2001. It is a crossbreeding of cold-tolerant species including Hitomebore and Kokuho Rose from California. **(3.4% market share)**

OTHER TYPES: Other types of rice not listed above make up **34.6% of the market in Japan.**

As you can see, the Koshihikari family leads the rice market of Japan.

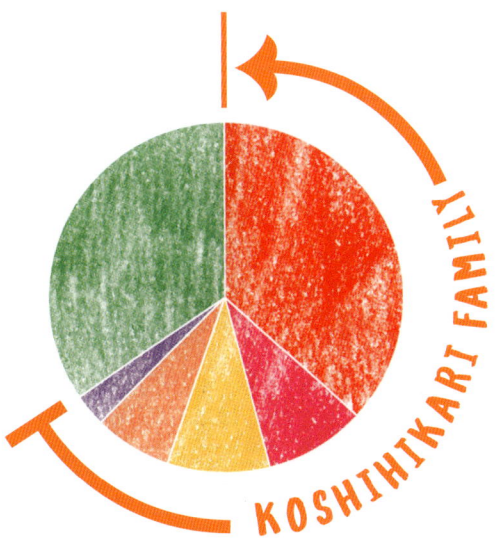

■	**KOSHIHIKARI**	36.1%
■	**HITOMEBORE**	9.7%
■	**HINOHIKARI**	9.0%
■	**AKITAKOMACHI**	7.2%
■	**NANATSUBOSHI**	3.4%
■	**OTHER TYPES**	34.6%

ABOUT RICE

JAPONICA IN THE U.S.

In the U.S., we can get Japonica rice at major supermarkets and Asian grocery stores. Here are some types you may see available.

SUPER-PREMIUM GRADE

KOSHIHIKARI: Because of its excellence, this rice has recently become widely harvested and distributed in the U.S. Shoppers may find it hard to tell that it's Koshihikari because many distributors feature a brand name more prominently than the Koshihikari name, such as Tamaki Gold (by Wismettac Asian Foods, Inc.), Nozomi (by JFC International, Inc.) or Matsuri (by Mutual Trading Co., Inc.). Some Japanese-grown Koshihikari can be found in limited supply at Japanese grocery stores in Hawaii, California and New York.

TAMANISHIKI: This is the brand name of JFC's original rice blend. It is a combination of Koshihikari and Yumegokochi, an advanced species of Koshihikari with less amylose.

AKITAKOMACHI: Recently gaining popularity in the U.S., this type is now harvested domestically. It is sold as Tamaki Classic (by Wismettac). Japan-grown Akitakomachi is available at some limited locations.

PREMIUM GRADE

NISHIKI: An original American rice from California. Exclusively distributed by JFC.

KOKUHO ROSE: An American rice bred by a Japanese agricultural entrepreneur, Mr. Keizaburo Koda, after WWII.

REGULAR GRADE

CALROSE: An American rice from California. The big distributors sell it under their own brand names, such as Diamond (by Farmers' Rice Cooperative), Botan (by JFC) and Hinode (by SunFoods, LLC).

WHAT MAKES TASTY RICE?

Whether a rice tastes good is related to its texture—specifically its fluffiness and stickiness. These qualities can be measured by calculating the amount and ratio of protein, amylose and amylopectin in the rice grains.

The protein content affects the hardness of the cooked rice. Protein is not water soluble, and it prevents rice grains from absorbing water. Therefore, lower protein content means better rice texture. For example, the super-premium Koshihikari brown rice has a protein content of about 6%, and the protein content of other high-grade rice is also 6 to 7%. The average protein content of a typical standard-grade rice is 7.4%. The less protein in the rice, the fluffier it becomes when cooked. Hard rice happens when the grains have a high protein content.

Now let's talk about the stickiness of rice. The starch in rice is composed of two molecules, amylose and amylopectin, and the balance between them determines the stickiness. When rice grains have less amylose (and more amylopectin), they become stickier after cooking. Rice with more amylose (like long-grain rice) is less sticky. For example, Japonica rice generally contains 17 to 27% amylose (the rest is amylopectin), while Indica has 27 to 31%. Mochi rice (sticky rice) has no amylose. Among the premium rice varieties, Koshihikari contains about 16% amylose, which is considered a moderate level for this grade of rice. A new rice variety, Ayahime from Hokkaido, has only 8.7% amylose, which is the lowest level among Japanese rice varieties. The Ayahime rice is highly valued for retaining its stickiness, even when it is cold.

 AMYLOSE    AMYLOPECTIN

amylose
27%~31%

amylopectin
69%~73%

INDICA

amylose
17%~27%

amylopectin
73%~83%

JAPONICA

amylose
0%

amylopectin
100%

MOCHI

STICKINESS →

In short, tasty rice is fluffy and sticky, a result of containing less protein and less amylose. 🍙

WHICH RICE GRADE IS BEST FOR MUSUBI?

For tasty and fluffy musubi, you should use at least premium-grade rice. Super-premium grade is ideal because, owing to its lower amylose content, the rice grains naturally stick together, requiring only gentle pressure from your hands to mold it into the musubi shape.

ABOUT RICE

CHAPTER THREE

THINGS TO KNOW BEFORE COOKING RICE

Rice may seem very straightforward to prepare, especially since modern rice cookers are so easy to use and don't require you to watch them, but there are a few things to know about how cookers work, the moisture content of rice and the equipment that goes along with making rice that will help you make better rice. Better rice means tastier musubi!

TYPES OF RICE COOKERS

Rice cookers are readily found at big-box stores, large appliance shops and Asian supermarkets, and an even wider selection is available at online shopping sites. Most are manufactured by American, Japanese, Chinese or Korean home appliance makers. The differences between cookers primarily come down to price, appearance and functions.

On the high end, expensive "Micom" models have a microcomputer that uses "fuzzy logic" technology to automatically adjust cooking temperature and time and offer multiple warming or cooking functions. Less-advanced models have only a single cooking mode and can be very inexpensive.

SUPER HIGH-END MODELS:

Micom-controlled with advanced multiple functions including high pressure, induction heating (IH) and a variety of rice-cooking modes. Typically costs $400 to $500 for a five-cup rice cooker. The lid is extremely solid, and the pot inside is very thick and made of premium materials.

HIGH-END MODELS:

Micom-controlled with multiple functions including IH and a variety of rice-cooking modes. Typically costs $300 to $400 for a five-cup rice cooker. The lid is extremely solid, and the pot inside is very thick and made of premium materials.

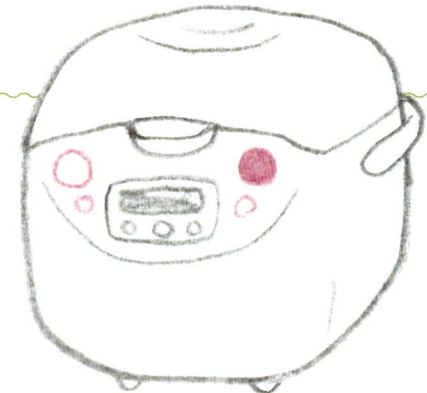

UPPER MODELS:

Micom-controlled with a basic variety of rice cooking modes. The lid is solid, and the rice pot inside is thick. Typically costs $100 to $200 for a five-cup rice cooker.

MIDDLE MODELS:

Simply designed, with a single cooking mode. May offer some additional basic functions like a warming setting. Although the lid is still solid, the rice pot inside is thin. Typically costs $50 to $100 for a five-cup rice cooker.

STANDARD MODELS:

Simply designed, with single cooking mode and no extra functions. Usually, the lid is a separate, completely removable piece made of thin glass or stainless steel. Typically priced at less than $50 for a five-cup rice cooker.

For the best quality rice, upper models or better are ideal because the microcomputer carefully controls the rice cooking process. One caution, though: the super high-end models, which use pressure cooking, sometimes crush the rice, depending on the water content of the uncooked rice. For regular home cooking, a high-end model is probably the best choice.

WATER IS IMPORTANT!

The water content in each rice grain depends on the species, the production method and the season. Right out of the bag, it will vary. So, before you press the START button on the cooker, you must be careful when measuring water to add to the pot. Here are some factors to consider.

REGIONAL DIFFERENCES

If the rice cooker is manufactured in Japan, by Japanese appliance makers, the water lines marked on the rice pot are intended for the rice produced in Japan. There is a clear difference between American-grown rice and Japanese rice: U.S. rice is much drier than Japanese rice, even though the species is same. For instance, California Koshihikari and Japanese Koshihikari have different water content. In general, when cooking American-grown rice in a Japanese-made cooker, 10% more water should be added. For example, to cook three cups of rice, you should fill water not to the "3" mark, but to 10% higher, approximately where 3.3 would be.

SEASONAL DIFFERENCES

Rice is harvested between late summer and early autumn. Right after harvest, rice grains contain quite a bit of water. As time goes by, the water content gradually decreases. The water content of rice sold in October (the

THE MUSUBI BOOK

rice bag sometimes will have a "New Crop" label) is vastly different from rice available the following summer. The rice sold in July will be much drier than what was available nine months ago. For better-quality cooked rice, you should adjust the amount of water for the season. Add about 5% more water for rice purchased when it is drier. For example, if you are using American rice in a Japanese pot, during the fall you would add 10% more water to compensate for the origin of the rice. (That would be to the 3.3 level in our example of three cups of rice.) In the summer, you would add an extra 5%, for a total of 15% more water (up to the 3.45 level), to make up for the drier rice.

MEASURING CUPS

Most new rice cookers come with a measuring cup. As you may have noticed, it is quite a bit smaller than regular measuring cups for cooking or baking. That is because, historically, for rice, one cup is equal to 180ml (approximately six ounces), whereas a standard American cup measure is eight ounces (approximately 240ml). Use the provided cup to measure your rice; that is how the water lines inside the pot are calibrated.

RICE PADDLES

A rice paddle is truly a very important cooking tool for making musubi. The freshly cooked rice is extremely hot (more than 200°F!) and shouldn't be touched with your bare hands.

A good rice paddle enables you to control the extra-steamy, delicate cooked rice as easily as if you were using your fingers. A bad rice paddle will make you lose control over the rice, sticking to the rice and smashing it.

HERE ARE THE IDEAL CHARACTERISTICS FOR A RICE PADDLE.

MATERIAL: Nonstick plastic

THICKNESS: As thin as possible

SURFACE: Full of tiny projections

GRIP: A flat face is better than a cylindrical shape to keep your wrist and fingers relaxed

Wooden rice paddles (including bamboo rice paddles) look natural and fancy, but are never recommendable. Rice constantly sticks to the wood.

When you buy a new rice cooker, the manufacturer often provides you with a free plastic rice paddle with tiny bumps on the surface. Most of these are not too bad, but they usually are not as thin as is desired.

THE MUSUBI BOOK

In my professional experience, the best paddle sold in the U.S. is commonly available at many megastores and drugstores for just $2 to $3.

When caring for your rice paddle, wash it with a sponge or cloth—the nonstick plastic is a soft material and is easily damaged. Never use a brush or steel wool to clean it. The surface of the paddle must be kept smooth for better control of the rice. 🍙

WHY IS AMERICAN RICE SO DRY?

Because of Japan's devoted rice culture, all the farmers, distributors and retailers pay utmost attention to quality control. They treat rice as a perishable product and store it under consistent temperature and humidity conditions all year, and polish the grains immediately before sale. (Japanese customers look for the polish date, which is imprinted on the bag.) All of this means that Japanese-produced rice is very consistent in quality, and efforts are made to ensure it does not dry out. In America, rice is considered a shelf-stable, nonperishable product. U.S. producers polish their rice much earlier before sale, and it is not stored as consistently, resulting in grains with less water content.

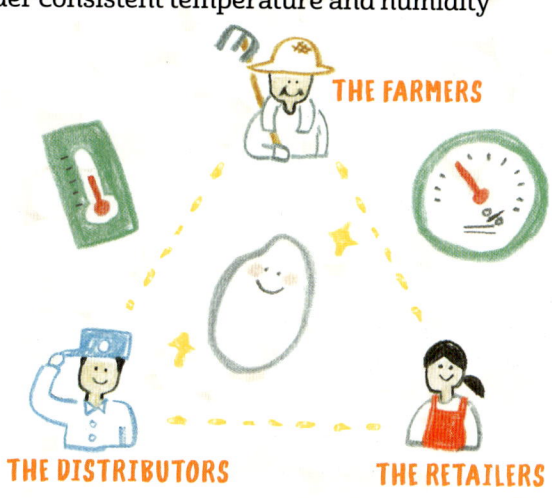

THE FARMERS

THE DISTRIBUTORS   THE RETAILERS

MADE IN JAPAN

THINGS TO KNOW BEFORE COOKING RICE

CHAPTER FOUR

HOW TO MAKE THE BEST RICE FOR MUSUBI

Now that you know what to use to make tasty rice, here are some tips on how to make the best rice to make musubi.

ALWAYS USE FRESHLY COOKED RICE!

Immediately after cooking, each rice grain contains a lot of steam.

Then, as the temperature in the rice cooker cools, the steam naturally and slowly changes to water. Although the interior temperature still seems very hot, the rice grains' texture is steadily changing, growing soggy.

Think of it this way: Imagine a sponge in a steamer with a heavy lid.

SPONGE = RICE

While it's on, the temperature inside the steamer should be slightly over 212°F, and the sponge is holding the maximum amount of steam it can contain.

Then, once you turn off the power, the temperature begins falling. As the temperature falls and the lid still covers the pot, the steam cannot escape. It changes to water inside the steamer. The steam inside the sponge also gradually changes to water.

Finally, all the steam becomes water. Everything—the inside of the steamer and the sponge—becomes completely soaking wet.

O.K., now, let's change some factors.

Let's remove the sponge right after the steamer is turned off. Because it is out in the open, the steam naturally evaporates from the sponge into the air. By the time the temperature of the sponge cools to the same as the room, a lot of water (as steam) has left the sponge, so the sponge is not soaking wet, only damp.

In the same way, if you leave the rice inside the rice cooker after it finishes cooking, the steam cannot escape from the enclosed space.

Even if left on the "keep warm" setting, the cooker does not maintain the same temperature it rises to when it cooks the rice. Accordingly, the temperature drops and steam starts changing to water, little by little.

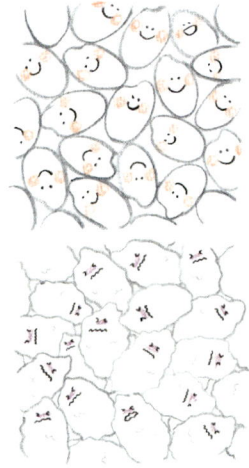

As the steam contained inside the rice grains becomes water, the cells of each grain's surface begin to collapse. They are no longer distinct grains, and they start to stick together. Now you have soggy rice. Musubi made from soggy rice is so watery, it lacks flavor. The soggy texture interrupts the harmony between rice and filling. It also sometimes makes us choke because of its unexpected stickiness.

To avoid musubi disaster, here are three important tips:

Tip #1: Use freshly cooked rice!

As soon as the rice is cooked, immediately transfer the rice to a bowl to release the excess steam into the air. The sooner you do this, the hotter the rice is and more steam can escape the rice grain.

Tip #2: When shaping the musubi, handle the rice as gently as possible. Use a rice paddle and a musubi mold.

Freshly cooked rice is too hot and delicate for our hands to handle well. Each rice grain is so fragile; it can be easily crushed. For these reasons, don't grab the rice with your hands (the way a sushi chef makes sushi). Instead, use a rice paddle and a mold to make to make musubi.

Tip #3: Never smash the rice!

You must pay special attention not to smash the rice grains. Always keep in mind that freshly cooked rice will naturally stick together as it cools down and releases excess steam. To help this process along effectively, you need to make as much space as possible between each rice grain. This gives the steam an escape route. If you apply too much pressure to the rice, there will be no space between grains, which forces the steam to remain in the rice as it cools down. Then it will become just a chunk of soggy rice. 🍙

INSIDE THE RICE POT

If you have ever used an electric rice cooker, you may have noticed that the texture of the cooked rice varies depending on its location inside the rice pot.

Vertically
The rice at the bottom is the wettest and stickiest. The rice on the surface is driest.

Horizontally
The rice toward the center is the wettest. Farther from the center, the rice is drier.

It is important to gently mix the rice together after it has cooked. That way, the texture and wetness of the rice is consistent throughout. If you allow it to sit too long without mixing, the grains will stick together and harden in position. Your rice will be a mix of wet-and-sticky and hard-and-dry in different places, which is very unappealing.

CHAPTER FIVE

LET'S MAKE FILLINGS!

Before the rice is cooked, we need to prepare our musubi fillings.

In a musubi, rice plays the starring role. The fillings should not overwhelm the rice in amount or flavor. They should play a supporting role to complement the taste of the main character, rice. Since only a small amount will be used, the fillings need to have a strong flavor. A filling that is too weak won't bring out the flavor of rice, and the musubi will taste bland. In other words, a salty filling should seem a bit too salty if we ate it alone. Think of the saltiness of bacon or prosciutto. That is the right intensity level for a musubi filling.

UME

SHAKE

OKAKA

TARAKO

KOMBU TSUKUDANI

TUNA-MAYO

MENTAIKO

THE MUSUBI BOOK

SHRIMP TEMPURA
(TEN-MUSU)

SPAM® MUSUBI

PORTUGUESE SAUSAGE

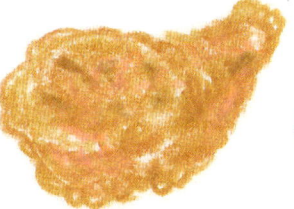
FRIED CHICKEN

BACON

HAM & CHEESE

TACO

LET'S MAKE FILLINGS!

UME

TRADITIONAL JAPANESE MUSUBI FILLINGS

Here are the five most common traditional musubi fillings. These days, it is fairly easy to find these ingredients at large supermarkets or Asian grocery stores.

UME

Ume, properly called umeboshi, is pickled plum. It is a naturally preserved traditional Japanese food. The taste is very sour and salty with no sweetness, and its plum flavor is not so strong as the Chinese *li hing mui*. Ume originated as a homemade preserve in rural Japan, but due to the complex procedure involved in making it, today it is mostly produced by factories.

There are two different types of ume. The first type of ume is drier, and the texture is soft. The other type is crunchy and juicy. In Japan, the first type is considered better and more authentic. Ume is often sold with the seed pit still inside. For musubi, you should remove the seed—it is very hard and you could crack a tooth if you bit into it!

SHAKE

Shake (salmon; pronounced shah-kay) is a very common and popular filling because it pairs so well with rice. Customarily, in Japan, half-dried salted salmon called *shiojake* is used for musubi. Shiojake is a traditional method of preservation from Northern Japan where they have long, cold winters. These days, while grilled shiojake is still very common, other salmon preparations that have a milder flavor and less saltiness are gaining popularity. Salmon flakes, made from fresh salmon with basic Japanese seasonings such as salt, *sake* and *mirin* (sweet rice wine), are one of these newer options. They're popular because factory-made salmon flakes are so convenient and available in inexpensive ($3 per small jar) to upscale ($20 per small jar) packages in grocery stores all over Japan.

So, for making salmon musubi, we have three options:

First, the traditional, grilled shiojake. Although it is very tasty with its rich flavor, it may be difficult to find outside of Japan, unless you are in a big city with a large Japanese population.

Second, grilling a piece of salmon you have seasoned heavily with salt and allowed to rest for an hour before cooking. This is the simplest preparation.

Third, making your own salmon flakes. For delicious homemade salmon flakes, mix together salt, sake, mirin and a pinch of sugar. Cover a couple raw salmon fillets with this mixture and slowly bake the salmon. It will cook into beautiful moist salmon flakes with no excess liquid. It may take 30 to 60 minutes, depending on the size of the fillets. When cooled, break into flakes. These will last three days in the refrigerator.

SHAKE

LET'S MAKE FILLINGS!

KATSUOBUSHI

OKAKA

Katsuobushi (shavings of dried bonito) is the most common ingredient in *dashi* (Japanese soup broth). It is also widely used as a garnish on many Japanese dishes to add rich flavor as well as a fancy appearance. This ingredient can be found easily not only at Asian grocery stores but also at major supermarkets. It is usually sold in small plastic packets, in a container of four to ten individual packets.

The musubi filling *okaka* is very easy to make. Just mix together katsuobushi, soy sauce and a touch of salt and sugar. If available, a little bit of mirin also helps to make the flavor richer. Be careful not to add too much liquid; you don't want the filling to be too watery.

TARAKO

Although fish eggs are very popular ingredients in Japanese cuisine, they are not so easy to get in most of the U.S., especially fresh ones. In particular, finding nice *tarako* (salted pollack roe) is much more difficult than obtaining *ikura* (salmon roe), which is popular for sushi. If you are fortunate enough to find good quality tarako, grill it until the skin is slightly burned. This preparation is very flavorful and is the perfect pairing for rice.

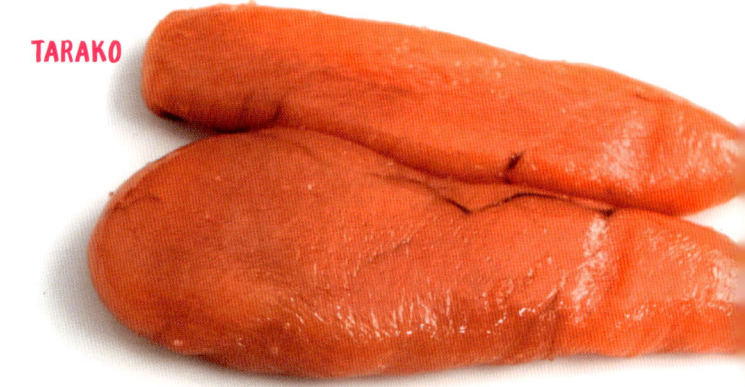

TARAKO

KOMBU TSUKUDANI

In its dried form, *kombu* seaweed is another common basic ingredient for making dashi. *Kombu tsukudani* is made by shredding the kombu and simmering it with sweetened shoyu. It is not something that is usually made at home, and is instead commercially produced, because it needs to cook for a very long time. It is a very traditional food and common not only as a musubi filling but also as a side dish or as a topping for plain rice (like ume) in a bento. You should be able to find it in Japanese markets or Asian grocery stores. To use it for musubi, no additional preparation is required. Just use a pinch of it directly from the package.

CONTEMPORARY JAPANESE MUSUBI

In Japan, there are many modern musubi fillings. Some have become more popular than the traditional fillings like ume or okaka. Three examples are tuna-mayo, *mentaiko* and shrimp *tempura*. Here's how you can prepare these most-popular choices at home:

TUNA-MAYO

TUNA

"Tuna-Mayo" is how Japanese refer to the most basic version of what Americans commonly call "tuna salad." The term is an abbreviation for canned tuna (albacore) and mayonnaise and it is considered a word in itself in Japanese. Tuna-mayo musubi are the permanent top seller among the incredible variety of musubi choices at Japanese 7-Eleven stores, which make up nearly one-third of the approximately 55,000 convenience stores in Japan, as of 2015.

LET'S MAKE FILLINGS!

The tuna-mayo mix for musubi is simple and easy for anyone to make: Combine canned (in water) solid albacore tuna (one 7-ounce can, drained, pressing to remove as much water as possible) with one teaspoon each of salt and sugar, and black or white pepper to taste. Mix everything together, breaking up the chunks of tuna. Don't smash the tuna completely; keep some small chunky pieces for better texture. Then, add a moderate amount of mayonnaise and mix together. The amount of mayo to add is up to you, but the consistency should be like paste; not dry and not too mayonnaise-y. After mixing, cover the tuna-mayo with waxed paper or plastic wrap and let it sit at least one hour (ideally, more than half a day) to allow excess water to seep out. Drain it off before using the mixture.

When it comes to choosing the tuna, the Costco Kirkland brand of solid albacore in water is very good. If you use chunk tuna, use less seasoning than for solid.

MENTAIKO

Mentaiko is spicy marinated pollack roe, and a very popular side dish for white rice. Unfortunately, you can hardly find it at American supermarkets, but it is usually sold at Japanese or Korean grocery stores. While the Korean version of mentaiko (called *myeongranjeot*) is very spicy and well fermented, with a strong seafood flavor, the Japanese version is mild, less fermented and very similar to plain salted pollack roe (tarako, mentioned in the previous section). For musubi, the Japanese version is preferable.

Mentaiko musubi are very popular at convenience stores in Japan. While tarako is usually grilled before using it in musubi, mentaiko is generally used without any

MENTAIKO

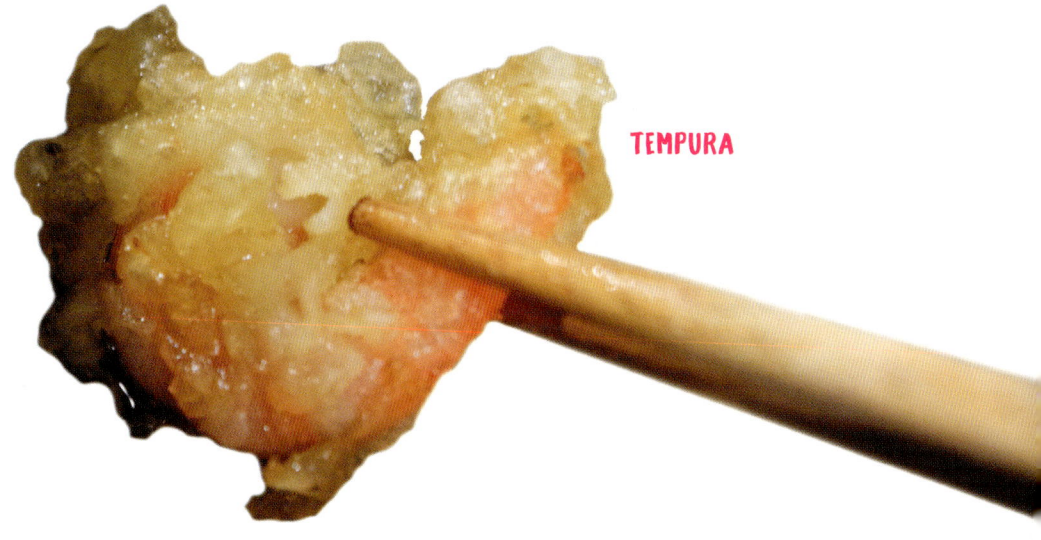

TEMPURA

cooking. Therefore, mentaiko musubi are not suitable for the original purpose of musubi, a portable form of preserved food, but they make a good takeout snack to eat right away.

SHRIMP TEMPURA (TEN-MUSU)

Tempura is a musubi filling that is gaining in popularity. In particular, a variety filled with small, white-shrimp tempura with a sweet shoyu sauce has recently spread all over Japan. It was originally produced as a staff meal at a tempura restaurant in a town called Tsu after World War II. It soon became a regular menu item called *ten-musu*. This regional specialty musubi was brought to its neighbor city, Nagoya (the fourth largest city, located in the middle of Japan), in the 1980s where it was seen on television food shows, rapidly becoming copied throughout the country.

To make ten-musu, make the small white-shrimp tempura on your own, or use frozen shrimp tempura. Make the sweet sauce by combining two tablespoons each of shoyu and sugar (and, optionally, well-boiled sake,

UME

SHAKE

KOMBU TSUKUDANI

TUNA-MAYO

OKAKA

TARAKO

MENTAIKO

SHRIMP TEMPURA (TEN-MUSU)

LET'S MAKE FILLINGS!

which makes it taste better). Lightly dip the tempura into the sauce. After the tempura batter has thoroughly absorbed the sauce, you can use it as a musubi filling.

AMERICAN FAVORITES FOR MUSUBI

Ever since musubi were brought to America by Japanese immigrants in the mid-nineteenth century, the fillings inside have gradually evolved. With the growth of Japanese-American food culture, you will find unique musubi all across America, suited to the different ingredients and tastes of the country! Some popular American varieties are SPAM®, Portuguese sausage, bacon, fried chicken, or ham and cheese.

SPAM®

SPAM® MUSUBI

SPAM® is the most famous ingredient for musubi in America. It is believed to have been created in Hawaii, on the island of Kauai. (See sidebar for more history.) Today, SPAM® musubi—instantly recognizable by their rectangle shape, topped with a slice of SPAM®—are one of the most-loved local snacks among Hawaii's population.

There are two ways to prepare SPAM® for musubi: plain or teriyaki-seasoned.

BACON

The plain version is quite simple. Just fry a piece of SPAM® in a pan. Since SPAM® contains plenty of salt, there is no need to add more. For adults, adding a bit of black pepper or chili pepper will add extra flavor.

The teriyaki version needs a little more preparation. The easiest method is to add soy sauce and sugar to the pan to coat the SPAM® as it fries. If you would like to make it even more flavorful, add mirin or sake in addition to the soy sauce and sugar, simmer it for a while to reduce the liquid, and then fry the SPAM® until a nice, savory-sweet soy sauce aroma comes out.

You can also choose to make your musubi the familiar, rectangle shape, or use a traditional, triangle, musubi shape.

PORTUGUESE SAUSAGE

Portuguese sausage is a smoked pork sausage seasoned with garlic, paprika and other spices. Portuguese sausage is very common in Hawaii—and in other states with a history of Portuguese immigrants—and it is a very good combination with white rice and nori. Perfect for musubi!

To prepare it for musubi, just fry it in a pan until slightly burnt. You might add a bit of fresh dill pickle when assembling the musubi, to balance the oiliness of the sausage.

PORTUGUESE SAUSAGE

LET'S MAKE FILLINGS!

FRIED CHICKEN

BACON

Bacon is a very common ingredient, and it also works well with white rice and nori. The preparation is quite simple: just grill it. However, you do not want it crispy—it should be kept tender to match the texture of the rice. If you like, you can sprinkle some black pepper to season it.

FRIED CHICKEN

If you have fried chicken, please try it for musubi—it is delicious! If you like the flavor of mayonnaise, dip the fried chicken into mayo before you put it inside the musubi. As the popularity of the tuna-mayo variety shows, mayonnaise is an excellent hidden seasoning for musubi.

HAM & CHEESE

HAM & CHEESE

Fry a piece of ham in a pan, and immediately after it is done, turn off the heat and top the ham with cheese. Then, once the cheese has melted, put the ham and cheese inside the rice ball. Cheese is a good partner with white rice if there is a stronger item (such as ham or bacon) with it.

GLOBAL CUISINE MUSUBI

Many dishes and seasonings are suitable for musubi. Today, some Japanese mega-convenience store chains are expanding their networks in Asian countries, where they provide a variety of musubi made with local ingredients and seasonings. Many of those international ingredients and flavors are already common and readily available in America. All the fillings in this section are easy to make and would taste excellent in a musubi!

PORK WITH KIM CHEE

Fry tiny pieces of pork, seasoning lightly with salt, and add some *kim chee*. Continue to stir-fry together until all the liquid has evaporated.

CHAR SIU

KIM CHEE

LET'S MAKE FILLINGS!

CHAR SIU (CHINESE BBQ PORK)

Mince a small amount of *char siu* and a tiny slice of ginger together. Add a bit of soy sauce to accentuate the flavor. If you prefer a sweeter taste, add a little bit of honey or sugar to the mix.

SATAY (INDONESIAN/MALAYSIAN SKEWERED BBQ CHICKEN)

Prepared, frozen satay can be found in the grocery store. Follow the cooking instructions, remove the skewers and season lightly with salt and cayenne pepper to enhance the flavor. This extra seasoning is necessary because *satay* is too mild on its own to contrast harmoniously with white rice and nori.

TACO (MEXICAN GROUND BEEF AND CHEESE)

Cook ground beef with Mexican taco seasoning, and add some shredded cheese to make a paste-like mixture. If you like, add some dill pickle relish for more texture and rich flavor.

TACO

LET'S MAKE FILLINGS!

SPAM® MUSUBI

BACON

PORK WITH KIMCHEE

CHAR SIU

FRIED CHICKEN

HAM & CHEESE

SATAY

TACO

LET'S MAKE FILLINGS!

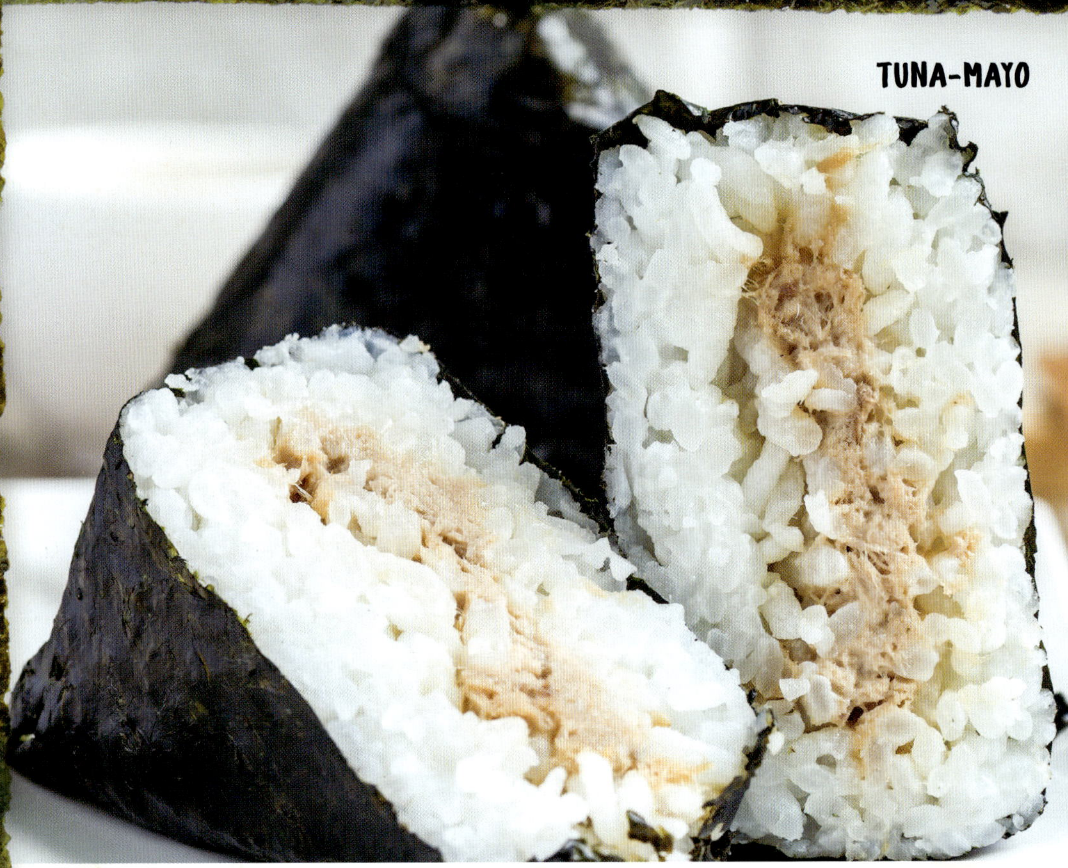

TUNA-MAYO

WHAT IS THE MOST POPULAR MUSUBI?

According to a 2015 poll by MyVoice Communications, Inc., one of the largest Japanese internet-based research firms, 33.7% of the 10,853 respondents answered that they "very much" like musubi; 62.4% answered that they "like" musubi; 2.7% said they "don't like" musubi very much and only 1.2% "dislike" it. In short, the vast majority (96.1%) of people enjoy musubi.

The same survey ranked the popularity of musubi fillings as follows:

1. Salmon (66.9% approval rating)
2. Tarako (48.7%)
3. Mentaiko (47.8%)
4. Tuna-Mayo (47.2%)
5. Kombu (42.2%)
6. Ume (41.1%)
7. Okaka (36.3%)

~~~~~~

Sales figures from convenience stores show a slightly different preference among their customers. According to the Institute of Onigiri Society, Japan's top three convenience store chains, 7-Eleven, Lawson and Family Mart, disclosed their musubi top sellers in 2014:

7-ELEVEN:
1. Tuna-Mayo
2. Salmon
3. Sekihan

LAWSON:
1. Tuna-Mayo
2. Kombu
3. Salmon Belly

FAMILY MART:
1. Salmon
2. Tuna-Mayo
3. Kombu

~~~~~~

Compared to the MyVoice general poll, Tuna-Mayo musubi stands out as a favorite at convenience stores, the largest musubi retail channel in Japan. Younger people are the primary customers at these locations, implying that this flavor is a favorite among that generation.

LET'S MAKE FILLINGS!

HAWAII'S ICONIC SPAM® MUSUBI

This musubi is reported to have been invented by a local-born Japanese nutritionist and entrepreneur, Ms. Barbara Funamura, of Kauai, Hawaii, and sold at a former Joni-Hana Hawaiian restaurant in the early 1980s. In Hawaii, locals like rice as well as SPAM®, and usually eat them together. One day, the idea to combine rice and a piece of SPAM® flashed into Mrs. Funamura's mind, and she acted. The first SPAM® musubi were triangular, and a piece of SPAM® was tucked inside the rice, just like traditional musubi. Later, Mrs. Funamura began making rectangular musubi, the same shape as a slice of SPAM®, by using a box-shaped mold. From Kauai, SPAM® musubi spread to Honolulu, Oahu, and gained popularity all over Hawaii.

Today, SPAM® musubi are sold at plate lunch and bento shops as well as convenience stores and grocery stores all over the Hawaiian Islands. Each SPAM® musubi costs around $1.50 to $2.50. They are enjoyed for breakfast, lunch, midday and nighttime snacks by everyone from preschoolers to senior citizens. New Yorkers are proud of their hot dogs, Philadelphia is known for cheesesteak, San Francisco has its famous clam chowder and Hawaii loves its SPAM® musubi!

CHAPTER SIX

LET'S MAKE MUSUBI!

Now that we know all about rice and we have prepared our fillings, we are ready to make musubi! Let's get started!

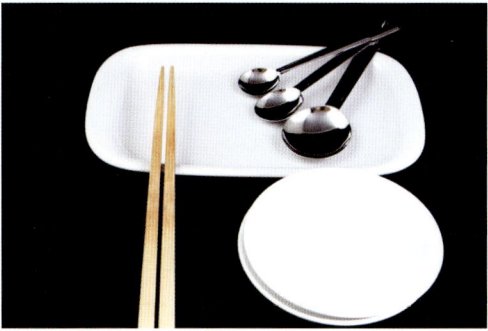

EQUIPMENT

Here are the tools you will need:

- Musubi Mold
- Cutting Board
  If you have an open-bottom mold, you will need a cutting board. If you use a small bowl or a mold with a bottom, you won't need one.
- Rice Paddle
- Plastic Bowl (medium size)
- Teaspoon (for adding your fillings)
- Chopsticks (for adding your filling)
- Baking Sheet or Tray
  (for your finished musubi)

LET'S MAKE MUSUBI!

INGREDIENTS

Assemble your ingredients before you begin.

Freshly cooked rice (see directions below and refer to Chapter Four for tips on making the best rice; one cup of raw rice usually yields enough rice to make three musubi)

Your favorite fillings (portioned out for each musubi)

Salt (Sea salt is highly recommended for the most harmony between rice and filling)

Nori (one-third sheet per each musubi)

MUSUBI MOLDS

A musubi mold sometimes comes in two parts, a part to hold the rice and a top to press it down. (We do not use the top press.) Many have no bottom. Occasionally, people make musubi using just their hands and fingers, without a mold. However, I recommend that you use a mold for these reasons:

- EASE—It is easier to make the proper musubi shape with a mold

- SAFETY—Avoid burning your hands on the hot rice

- CLEANLINESS—Not touching the rice with your hands is more hygienic

- TASTE—The rice stays fluffy because you handle it less

Musubi molds are readily available in America, sold at Japanese grocery stores and sometimes other Asian markets, and of course online shopping sites like Amazon.com. In Hawaii, they are found at almost any store with kitchenware.

The typical triangle, plastic cage-type molds cost only $3 to $5 each.

If you are unable to get a musubi mold, as an alternative, you may use any hand-sized bowl (around 3 to 3.5 inches in diameter) or baking mold with a depth of around 1.5 inches and sides that are as vertical as possible. If you use such an alternative circular mold, the rice ball will also be spherical when it comes out of the mold. Gently shape it into the proper triangular shape using your hands and fingers.

LET'S MAKE MUSUBI!

THE PROCEDURE

1. Cook your rice. First, rinse rice with water, washing it by hand. As the water turns milky, pour it out and replace with fresh water, and continue to wash. After three or four repetitions, the water should be slightly cloudy, but mostly clear. Add the correct amount of water for your rice cooker according to the measurements inside the pot, making adjustments as necessary, as covered in Chapter Four. Remember that since California rice is drier than Japanese rice, if you cook California rice in a Japanese-made rice cooker, you must add approximately 10% more than the mark. Press the START button to begin cooking.

2. If you are using a high-end model or better, it takes about an hour to cook the rice, because the rice cooker is smart enough to calculate the moisture in the dry rice and adjust temperature and cooking time. If you use a standard model, the cooker immediately starts heating the rice pot, and within 40 minutes, the rice should be cooked.

3. While you wait for the rice to cook, prepare your fillings and equipment. Cut your nori sheets into thirds and portion your fillings. Moisten the mold, cutting board and rice paddle. You don't want them dripping wet, but you want to make sure they are not completely dry so the rice doesn't stick. If your musubi mold has a press-top, you can set it aside. Pressing the musubi crushes the rice too much.

4. Immediately after the rice finishes cooking, transfer the very hot, steamy rice to your plastic bowl. You need four ounces of cooked rice per musubi.

5. Very gently, use the rice paddle to break apart the rice in the bowl. Depending on where the rice was in the pot as it cooked, it may be firmer or softer than other parts. (See sidebar, Chapter Four.) You want to mix the rice together evenly so that the texture of each bite is consistent.

6. If you are using a bottomless mold, set it on the cutting board. If you are using a bowl or mold with a bottom to shape your musubi, you don't need the board.

7. Using the rice paddle, carefully and gently put the steamy rice into the mold. Fill it less than 40% full. IMPORTANT: Never push hard on the rice; gently guide it into place to allow for space between each rice grain. As covered in Chapter Four, the open space between grains is very important to release excess steam from the super-hot rice.

8. Add your favorite filling on top of the rice, positioned in the center of the mold.

9. Cover your filling with another scoop of steamy rice. Fill the mold so the rice comes to just above the top. Remember: NEVER SMASH THE RICE! Allow the rice grains to "breathe."

10. Spread a pinch of salt evenly over the palms of your hands.

NEVER SMASH THE RICE!

LET'S MAKE MUSUBI!

RECTANGULAR MUSUBI MOLDS FOR SPAM® MUSUBI

When you are shopping for your musubi mold, you may also find another shape of mold which is rectangular instead of triangular. This type is especially designed for SPAM® musubi.

SPAM® musubi were triangular, like all other musubi, when they first were invented. However, because of the rectangular shape of a slice of SPAM®, people started using rectangular molds to make the process easier, and it caught on. Today, most SPAM® musubi are rectangular, and the molds to make them are easily found in retail stores.

An interesting aspect of the SPAM® musubi mold is that its purpose is not to create a fluffy-rice musubi, but to press the rice into a solid form together with a non-sticky slice of SPAM®. Because of this mold, the musubi becomes dense, heavy and sometimes mushy. In truth, it may need to be regarded as another variety of musubi, different from the traditional soft musubi, more like pressed sushi (*oshi-zushi*), a concept that is closer to sandwiches than to musubi. The latest new musubi invention, *onigirazu*, follows this trend.

ONIGIRAZU

11. Slowly remove the hot rice ball from the mold. Be careful not to crush it; it is still extremely fragile.

12. Carefully hold the rice ball with your fingers, place it on a single palm and very gently roll it between your palms and fingers. Do this very quickly—within just two to three seconds. It is very important that you do not squeeze the rice. The purpose of this step is to lightly salt the plain rice, as well as to make the surface of the rice a bit smoother.

ADVANCED MUSUBI-MAKING SKILL!

If you are experienced, you may be able to shape the rice into a nice triangle, even without a mold, by controlling your finger movements.

LET'S MAKE MUSUBI!

13. Gently place the fragile rice ball on a baking sheet, flat side down, and leave it for 10 minutes until the surface is cool and all the steam has escaped. Then, turn it over, and wait for another 10 minutes to allow the other side to cool.

14. Now the rice has cooled down and has a good level of moisture. Without so much steam, the rice grains can stick together better. The rice ball is no longer so fragile and will hold its shape well.

15. Last step! With the nori positioned the long way pointing away from you, place the rice ball on the upper or lower half. (It doesn't matter which side, but it should not be in the center.) The flat bottom of the triangle should be closest to the center. Gently fold the other half around it to wrap completely. Now, it can stand on its own. It is officially a musubi! 🍙

CHAPTER SEVEN

BEYOND BASIC MUSUBI
(MIXED RICE AND PILAF)

Musubi are not limited to the traditional combination of white rice, filling and nori. Various kinds of mixed rice and pilafs have strong potential to add flavor and visual variety to musubi. The assembly portion for these kinds of musubi, where the flavor is already in the rice itself, is much easier because you do not need to put fillings inside the rice! Following are examples of the kinds of fancy-looking and tasty musubi you can make for your family.

MIXED RICE MUSUBI

Mixed-rice musubi are made with rice that has been combined with flavorful ingredients before being molded.

Prepare your equipment the same as for regular musubi. In addition, prepare a bowl of salted water. The level of saltiness should be like sea water.

Mixed-rice musubi are made the same way as regular musubi, only without the extra step of adding fillings between two layers of rice: Add the mixed rice into the mold, filling it to the top. Remember: Don't crush the rice! Wet your hands with salt water, carefully remove the rice from the mold and gently finish shaping the warm, fragile rice ball with your hands and fingers. As with the white rice musubi, set your finished musubi on a tray to cool down for 10 minutes per side. You do not need to wrap mixed-rice musubi with nori.

One cup of uncooked rice yields enough to make three musubi.

Kombu Rice

INGREDIENTS
- Kombu tsukudani
- Rice
- White sesame seeds

Mince kombu tsukudani (pieces should be cut shorter than ¼-inch). Combine one tablespoon of minced kombu with one teaspoon of white sesame seeds per musubi and mix together with just-cooked white rice. Mix quickly but gently with a rice paddle, being careful not to smash the rice. If you like, you may season lightly with salt and/or sugar.

Bacon & Almond Rice

INGREDIENTS

Bacon
Rice
Sea-salted almonds
Black pepper

Mix hot white rice with bacon crumbles and slices of lightly sea-salted almonds. Use one tablespoon of each per musubi. If you like, you can put in a bit of black pepper to add an extra flavor kick.

Edamame & Ume Rice

INGREDIENTS
Edamame
Rice
Ume
White sesame seeds

Boil frozen edamame (soybeans) for two minutes in heavily salted water. While the edamame cook, remove the seeds from the ume and mince the ume meat. Use one ume and 10 edamame per musubi. Mix the soybeans and ume with hot white rice, sprinkle one teaspoon of white sesame seeds per musubi and sprinkle lightly with sea salt to taste.

Edamame & Cheese Rice

INGREDIENTS
Frozen edamame
Rice
Cheddar cheese
Sea salt

Boil frozen edamame for two minutes in heavily salted water. While the soybeans cook, dice cheddar cheese into ¼-inch cubes. Mix edamame, cheese and hot rice together and season to taste with sea salt. You will need 10 edamame and 10 cheese cubes per musubi.

Salmon Rice

INGREDIENTS
- Salmon fillet
- White sesame seeds
- Sea salt
- Salmon skin (optional)

Break apart a broiled salmon fillet into flakes, and microwave it until the meat becomes a little dry. Per each musubi, combine two tablespoons salmon flakes, a teaspoon of white sesame seeds and a pinch of sea salt with hot white rice. Be careful not to over mix, because it makes the rice greasy.

If the salmon is skin-on, broil the skin well until it is very crisp, mince it, and mix it together with the salmon flakes and rice. The addition of the crispy skin makes it even more flavorful.

PILAF MUSUBI

Pilaf is rice that has been cooked with broth or other flavorful liquids instead of plain water. These musubi also have additional ingredients that are added before the rice is molded.

Prepare your equipment the same as for regular musubi. In addition, prepare a bowl of salted water. The level of saltiness should be like sea water.

Just like mixed-rice musubi, pilaf musubi are made the same way as regular musubi, only without the extra step of adding fillings between two layers of rice. Add the pilaf rice into the mold, filling it to the top. Remember: Don't crush the rice! Wet your hands with salt water, carefully remove the rice from the mold and gently finish shaping the warm, fragile rice ball with your hands and fingers. Set your finished musubi on a tray to cool down for 10 minutes per side. You do not need to wrap pilaf musubi with nori.

Sekihan (Japanese Red Bean Rice)

INGREDIENTS
- Azuki beans
- Black rice
- White rice
- Mochi rice
- Black sesame seeds

Sekihan is a very traditional dish made to celebrate special occasions, such as welcoming the New Year, weddings and birthdays. The cooking is easy, the appearance is fancy, and it is very simple and tasty.

This recipe makes 8 or 9 finished musubi. Gently boil ½ cup of azuki beans and 2 teaspoons of black rice with 1 cup of water for 20 minutes. Strain out the beans and rice, saving the purple-colored water.

Mix 1½ cups each of white rice and mochi rice, wash thoroughly and drain in a sieve. Add the rice and purple water to the rice cooker. Add more plain water as needed to fill the pot to the level for 3 cups of mochi rice. (Consult your rice cooker for guidelines.) Add the azuki beans, black rice, 1 teaspoon of sea salt and begin cooking.

In higher-grade rice cookers, mochi rice cooks much faster than regular white rice. Cooking will be done in about 40 minutes. After the sekihan is cooked, transfer it to a larger bowl right away. The azuki beans and the black rice usually rise to the top; mix them in gently to combine evenly. Be very careful — mochi rice is extremely delicate and easily smashed.

Once you have shaped your rice, you may sprinkle a pinch of black sesame seeds over the surface of the musubi.

Chinese Fried Rice Flavor

INGREDIENTS

Chicken stock
or Chinese-style
chicken soup

Char siu

Scrambled egg

Green peas

Black pepper
to taste

Sesame oil

It is almost impossible to make musubi from fried rice. This is because the oil prevents the rice grains from sticking to each other, so the musubi does not hold together. But, never give up! This musubi uses a Chinese pilaf and tastes like fried rice.

Cook rice using salted chicken broth or stock, instead of plain water. The broth should be slightly saltier than the level of saltiness you would enjoy in a soup. If you can get Chinese-style chicken soup, that is even better! While the rice cooks, mince a lean portion of char siu—you will need 3 tablespoons of minced char siu per cup of raw rice. Use a non-stick pan and scramble an egg with no oil.

As soon as the pilaf is cooked, transfer it to a large bowl and mix it with the char siu, scrambled egg and 3 tablespoons of green peas. Add black pepper to taste and only a few drops of sesame oil (too much will prevent the rice from holding together), then gently mix everything together.

Curry Pilaf

INGREDIENTS

Chicken stock or broth

Minced meat (optional)

Small pieces of vegetables (optional)

Minced meat (optional)

Curry powder

Paprika to taste

Black, white or cayenne pepper to taste

Cook rice using salted chicken broth or stock, instead of plain water. The broth should be slightly saltier than the level of saltiness you would enjoy in a soup. In addition, you may add any kind of minced (or ground) meat, small pieces of vegetables (corn, diced carrot, etc.) and spices (curry, paprika, pepper). For each cup of raw rice, use 1 teaspoon of curry powder and 3 tablespoons of mix-ins. You will be able to make three musubi from this amount of rice. Use slightly less liquid than when cooking rice in plain water, because some extra liquid will come out from the meat and vegetables.

Immediately after the curry pilaf is cooked, transfer it to a large bowl, sprinkle seasonings to taste, and gently mix the rice. For a spicier taste, you can add up to 50% more curry powder, as well as using white and/or cayenne pepper.

BEYOND BASIC MUSUBI

NORI OR NO NORI?

Mixed-rice and pilaf musubi often are not wrapped with nori. Filled musubi are almost always nori-wrapped. Typically, musubi are wrapped in nori immediately after they have cooled down, but there is another option: Wrap your musubi with nori as you eat them!

Here are the pros and cons of the two methods:

	PRE-WRAPPED	WRAPPED WHILE EATING
PROS:	• Easy to pack and eat • Consistent shape	• Nori is crisp, with strong flavor
CONS:	• Nori gets soggy and flavorless	• Expensive to pack—everything must be packed separately • Without nori, the musubi falls apart more easily

In Japan, musubi—especially homemade ones—are most likely to be wrapped with nori before being packed, because it is more convenient and practical. The triangle-shaped musubi wrapped with nori is a cultural icon, so no matter if it impacts the quality, Japanese people feel that is how a musubi should be. Still, for some special occasions, like bringing musubi for potluck parties, the fun and freshness of assembling the musubi just before eating is a great idea!

CHAPTER EIGHT

MUSUBI ON THE GO!

Musubi are a perfectly portable food, but they require special care in packing. Commercially sold musubi are most commonly wrapped in cellophane. Home cooks can choose from several options for materials. Don't worry, it's easy to do!

HOW TO PACK YOUR MUSUBI

Because the cooked rice retains moisture, the surface of each musubi is slightly damp. Unlike sandwiches, musubi will stick together if they touch, which can be annoying when you try to grab one!

To avoid this irritating problem, and to help protect the musubi, you should separate each musubi when you pack them or put them out for your friends and family to eat. You don't always need to wrap each one completely, but some sort of divider should be used between them. For example, if you are serving the musubi for a party, a small piece of one of the following materials between each musubi is enough to keep them from sticking together, and the musubi will still be visible. When you put out a tray of musubi that includes some mixed-rice or pilaf varieties, the presentation is very cheerful, which will impress everyone!

There are three materials you could use:

Waxed paper is the best of these choices. Not only does it not stick to the rice or nori, it can slowly absorb excess water when the musubi are packed in a container. It is a breathable material and helps prevent the musubi and nori from getting too soggy.

Aluminum foil is the most commonly used wrapping material for homemade musubi in Japan because of its practicality. The sturdiness of aluminum foil helps the musubi to keep their shape, even if they are transported without a container—you can wrap up a musubi completely and take it to go in your bag without worrying it will be crushed or break!

Plastic wrap is not the best choice, although it can be convenient. Due to its thinness and flimsy structure, it's not a good choice to use as a divider between musubi. It is more useful when you need to completely wrap your musubi. However, it is so good at sealing everything in, the musubi and nori eventually get soggy from all the moisture.

Pack your basket with musubi and some snacks and drinks—let's go on a picnic! 🍙

MUSUBI ON THE GO!

GLOSSARY

AKITAKOMACHI — a Koshihikari crossbreed developed in Japan in 1984, designed for cold tolerance.

AMYLOPECTIN — one of the two molecules in rice starch (along with amylose), which affects stickiness. The more amylopectin, the stickier the rice.

AMYLOSE — one of the two molecules in rice starch (along with amylopectin), which affects stickiness. The more amylose the rice contains, the drier the texture of the rice.

AZUKI — a red bean widely harvested throughout East Asia. Azuki is usually simmered with sugar and used whole or mashed into paste. Azuki desserts are historically very popular both in Japan and China.

AZUKI

BENTO VARIETIES

BENTO — a packed-to-go lunch. A bento box generally includes white rice and several small portions of side dishes; other rice dishes—such as musubi or pilaf—or sandwiches, may be substituted for white rice. Bento can be homemade or are bought at grocery stores, supermarkets and depachika (basement-level department store food malls).

CALROSE — Calrose is a regular-grade, medium-grain rice developed in 1946 and commonly sold throughout the United States. The big distributors sell it under their own brand names, such as Diamond (by Farmer's Rice Cooperative), Botan (by JFC International, Inc) and Hinode (by SunFoods, LLC).

DASHI — a broth made from katsuobushi, dried kombu, *iriko* (dried sardine) and/or dried shiitake mushrooms. Dashi may be made from any of these ingredients individually or a combination, to make more rich and complex flavored dashi.

DEPACHIKA — the literal translation is "department store basement," a combined word from *depaato* (department store) and *chika* (basement). An enormous variety of quality delicatessens, bakeries, confectionaries and takeout restaurants occupy the depachika. Department stores in Japan compete to improve their depachika in order to attract more customers.

EDAMAME — young soybeans, prepared by boiling in salted water.

PHOTO AC

GLOSSARY

FURIKAKE

FURIKAKE — a dry seasoning mix, which is sprinkled over cooked rice. The taste is a little salty as well as sweet, and the flavor varies depending on the combination of the dried ingredients such as egg flakes, shaved bonito flakes, sesame seeds, shredded nori, etc. While it is usually eaten with white rice, it is also popular as a topping on deep-fried pork or chicken in Hawaii.

HINOHIKARI — a crossbreed of Koshihikari developed in Japan in 1989 as a warm-climate tolerant variety. It is commonly harvested in southwestern Japan from the Osaka area to Kyushu Island.

HITOMEBORE — a crossbreed of Koshihikari developed in Japan in 1991; a variety even more cold-tolerant than Akitakomachi.

IKURA — salmon roe preserved in salt or shoyu; a very common ingredient for sushi.

INDICA — one of the two big categories of rice in the world (cf. Japonica). Indica was genetically divided from Japonica in south or southeast Asia about 3,900 years ago. While the grain's shape is much longer and thinner than Japonica, it contains more protein and amylose, which makes its texture dry and crunchy.

JAPONICA — one of the two big categories of rice in the world (cf. Indica). It emerged about 8,000 to 9,000 years ago in ancient China. Short-grain rice and medium-grain rice belong to this category, which has a tender and sticky texture.

KATSUOBUSHI — smoked dried bonito. The hard, stone-like blocks are turned into flakes by using a special shaving device. "Katsuobushi" refers to both the block and flaked form. The flakes are traditionally used for dashi (broth), as well for toppings on various dishes and seasoned with soy sauce as a musubi filling.

KOKUHO ROSE — the first U.S. premium-grade, medium-grain rice, bred by a Japanese agricultural entrepreneur, Mr. Keizaburo Koda, in 1962.

KOMBU TSUKUDANI — a traditional, preserved accompaniment for cooked rice. To make tsukudani, small fish, seaweed or wild vegetables are simmered with soy sauce and sugar until the taste intensifies. Kombu seaweed is one of the most popular tsukudani items, especially for musubi and bento.

KOSHIHIKARI — the most harvested and consumed, super-premium, short-grain rice in Japan. The first version was developed in 1956, and several advanced Koshihikari and various new crossbreeds (such as Hitomebore, Hinohikari, and Akitakomachi) have been developed since. In America, Koshihikari is also harvested and widely distributed under different names like Tamaki Gold (by Wismettac Asian Foods, Inc.), Nozomi (by JFC International Inc.) or Matsuri (by Mutual Trading Co., Inc.).

KOMBU TSUKUDANI

MAKIZUSHI

MAKIZUSHI — rolled sushi, from *maki* (rolled). Typically, vinegar-seasoned rice and fillings (such as raw seafood, pickles or fresh vegetables) are rolled in a nori sheet, and served cut into bite-size pieces. The roll size varies from *hosomaki* (thin roll, 1.25-inch) to *futomaki* (thick roll, 2.50-inch). While hosomaki usually has only a single filling, futomaki uses several different fillings, which makes it more delicious and beautiful.

MICOM — a contraction of "microcomputer," a technology which has been widely used in home appliances for their smart operation such as auto-temperature adjustment.

MIRIN — sweet rice wine, often used for Japanese cooking to make the dish more mild and rich. (Not meant for drinking.)

THE MUSUBI BOOK

NORI

MOCHI RICE — another name for sweet rice. Because it is widely used for making mochi (Japanese rice cake), people prefer to call this type of rice mochi rice instead of sweet rice. It is actually not sweet, so that name is often confusing. It is also often referred to as sticky rice, due to its texture.

NANATSUBOSHI — the seventh generation of Koshihikari, created in 2001; has the strongest cold tolerance, a result of multiple crossbreedings with Hitomebore and California-born Kokuho Rose. It is mostly harvested in Hokkaido, the largest rice-producing region in Japan.

NISHIKI — a California-grown, premium-grade, medium-grain rice which is exclusively distributed by JFC International, Inc.

NORI — traditionally refers to edible algae (seaweed). Commonly refers to the dried sheets which are essential as a wrap for sushi and musubi. Although nori itself doesn't have a strong taste, its rich seaweed flavor accentuates the other ingredients. Pre-cut and seasoned nori is commonly found in small individual packets at grocery stores, and are popular as a snack item.

OKAKA — a traditional musubi filling made from shaved, dried bonito (katsuobushi), mostly seasoned with soy sauce.

OKAZUYA — Japanese delicatessen; the word is a combination of *okazu* (Japanese food) and *ya* (shop). Okazuya make and sell many varieties of Japanese foods and rice dishes (such as musubi and rolled sushi). Okazuya are common where Japanese Americans live, especially in Hawaii and California. Interestingly, the word is not commonly used in Japan because it sounds too general and vague.

ONIGIRAZU — A new style of musubi in Japan, originally introduced in a popular cooking *manga* (illustrated magazine) series in the early '90s and has grown in popularity since the mid-2010s. As the name implies (*azu* in Japanese means "not to do" in Japanese), it is the anti-musubi (or nigiri, the more common term in Japan). It resembles a Western-style sandwich, rather than a musubi rice ball. While it has many creative fillings (such as fresh lettuce), its popularity is still limited since it lacks many fundamental qualities that make musubi so appealing, such as portability, storage stability and the familiarity of quick home cooking.

OSHIZUSHI — simply translated to "pressed (*oshi*) sushi." One of the main forms of sushi, along with *nigirizushi* (the general term for traditional rolled sushi). Oshizushi is made by layering vinegar-seasoned white rice with slices of marinated seafood and pressing it all together. While nigirizushi has its origin in Tokyo, oshizushi is very common in Osaka (Kansai region).

PILAF — general name for a rice dish which is seasoned and cooked with various ingredients. There are many kinds of pilaf in the world, varying with each country's own ingredients and seasoning, for instance, jambalaya (Louisiana), *paella* (Spain) and *biryani* (India).

SAKE — used both as a general word for alcoholic beverages, but also refers to Japanese rice wine. Pronounced "sah-kay." In addition to the traditional alcoholic beverages, sake frequently plays a role as a seasoning of Japanese cuisine to add aroma flavor and subtle mildness.

SHAKE — salmon; pronounced "shah-kay." As one of the most popular musubi fillings, it is broiled or grilled with salt and some other supplemental seasoning such as rice wine, sugar, mirin, etc.

SUSHI

SHOYU — Japanese soy sauce, made with salted fermented soybeans and wheat. Compared to other Asian countries' soy sauce, shoyu generally stands out for its lightness and clarity of color, texture and taste.

SUSHI — a Japanese traditional rice dish. Although there are several styles, most sushi is served as a combination of some seafood or vegetable, on or in a small portion of vinegar-seasoned rice.

TAMANISHIKI — a brand name of blended rice consisting of California Koshihikari and Yumegokochi, which is globally distributed by JFC International.

TARAKO — pollack roe; *tara* (pollack) + *ko* (child, i.e. roe). In Japanese cuisine, it usually refers to pollack roe preserved in salt. A piece of grilled tarako is a common a musubi filling.

UME — plum. In Japanese cuisine, it refers to pickled plum, formally called umeboshi. There are two types of umeboshi. The traditional style is dried, a process which makes the meat tender. The other style is made without the drying process, and the final product is crunchy.

WASABI — Japanese horseradish, commonly used in a paste form as a condiment for *sashimi* (sliced raw fish), as well as sushi. Wasabi paste is traditionally made by grinding the root using a piece of dried shark skin, but manufacturers produce wasabi paste and dried wasabi powder for users' convenience.

THE MUSUBI BOOK

About the Author & Illustrator

MANABU ASAOKA

Manabu Asaoka is the owner and musubi culture evangelist of Mana-Bu's, a quality boutique musubi shop established in Honolulu, Hawaii, in 2008. Today, the shop has been renamed Mana Musubi, provided by Mana-Bu's.

In addition to his unique professional background as a hull insurance underwriter for 16 years in Tokyo, Manabu has a master's degree in communication from Hawaii Pacific University focusing on customer satisfaction in intercultural business environments. Together with his wife, Fumiyo, a licensed nutritionist, he chose to open a musubi shop, convinced it is the best medium to showcase authentic Japanese food culture to local American families. He is eager to spread Japanese musubi culture not just in Hawaii, but throughout the world, and believes in emphasizing the importance of home cooking and its role in creating strong family ties and healthy eating habits.

Manabu's enthusiasm and dedication to quality and top-notch customer service has made him a favorite in Hawaii's local food scene. Mana-Bu's has been the recipient of the "Hawaii's Best" Ilima Award, and featured nationally on Food Network and Travel Channel television programs. The shop produces 35 different types of musubi, including varieties made with brown rice and 10-grain rice, making a limited number of pieces each day, about 1,000, which are sold out by lunchtime.

MANABU AND FUMIYO

ABOUT THE AUTHOR & ILLUSTRATOR 107

MARIA

 **@maria_asaoka**

Maria Asaoka, Manabu's niece, is an up-and-coming illustrator based in Shizuoka, located in central Japan with fantastic views of Mt. Fuji.

She specializes exclusively in *yuru-kyara*, a contemporary Japanese drawing style of cute and unsophisticated characters. Yuru-kyara is synonymous with the representative mascots widely used by companies and local governments and organizations as emblems of their history, culture, philosophy or sense of values.

As early as her design school years, Maria's warm and fuzzy yuru-kyara drawings have been in the limelight, receiving several local and national awards. Today, as a professional illustrator, she seeks to hone her yuru-kyara drawing skills and put as much meaning as possible into her art, creating a single yuru-kyara to replace thousands of explanatory words, enabling communication beyond language barriers.

 **Mana-Bu's dba Mana Musubi**
1618 South King St., Honolulu, Hawaii 96826
www.hawaiimusubi.com